Simple Gold

Simple Gold

Musings of Mind and Spirit

J. MICHAELS

RESOURCE *Publications* · Eugene, Oregon

SIMPLE GOLD
Musings of Mind and Spirit

Resource Publications
An Imprint of Wipf and Stock Publishers
199 W. 8th Ave., Suite 3
Eugene, OR 97401

www.wipfandstock.com

ISBN 13: 978-1-60899-355-0

Manufactured in the U.S.A.

Dedicated to those who, despite the obvious,
insist on the divine reality

Contents

Preface

L IFE IS VERY SIMPLE. It originates from one Source from which it never leaves. It is fortified by an undeniable presence and an eternal property. It is freely given, sustained, and appreciated from its ever-beginning to its never-end. It is whole, free, peaceful, eternal, and joyous. It is also invisible; blinded to sight by the eyes, deafened from hearing by the ears, and obfuscated to the mind by perception. It is the greatest of gifts *and* tragedies. The nature of the gift is obvious, unless you happen to be a normal human being. The tragedy is that we don't know that it rests, extended, just beyond out grasp.

A few millennia ago, a rather significant event occurred. Call it The Fall, The Big Bang, or The Great Separation, or call it simply, the beginning of time. It was followed by another major event. Let's call that one The Great Forget. As our souls departed the eternal life in favor of an individuated and finite existence, it soon became obvious that we had screwed up royally! That realization was so overwhelming, so devastating, that we did what we do best in the material world, we forgot. When anything gets to be too much for us, we deny it. Either that or we project the guilt, fear, or rage associated with the event onto someone else; a brother turned convenient scapegoat. Having now adopted our universal coping strategy, one that *seems* to work both on the micro and macro levels, we were positioned to accept the grandest delusion ever perpetrated; that of denying our own Source, the One we left in regret and guilt so profound that we were unable to bear the acceptance of its *apparent* loss.

And so here we are, in a world we made as alternative; a tawdry substitute and separated from the Source of all there is. And the truly sad part is that we have been doing it for so long that we now faithfully, despite all of its rather formidable drawbacks, defend it to our dying breath. At the risk of appearing disparaging, let's take a look at what we have traded for the divine life described above. But where do we start? Do we start with the wars that have plagued us since *civilization* began? Or do we begin with the unending, yet futile, search for unity with another human body? Perhaps we should discuss the uneven distribution of wealth that is responsible for a world with extremely affluent individuals living alongside millions of starving poor. Or maybe it's the never-ending stream of new diseases and maladies that rob us of our health, our peace, and eventually our existence. We could mention the daily and persistent violence that ranges from child abuse, rape, murder, to mayhem in its almost endless variety that challenges our sanity to live among it. And yet with all of this, we not only create science and logic to validate and defend it, we cling desperately to it, even to our last breath. It is unthinkable to me that any sane person could accept this situation not only as the truth but as what we deserve. But guilt and fear are seemingly formidable enemies and both work in tandem to assure that we continue to do just that, accept such an inferior offering as the best we can do.

The good news is that it isn't the best we can do. The best we can do is what we gave up in exchange for belief in separation and the world that exemplifies that separation so well. Our self-inflicted guilt has formed into a wall of illusion that now shields a divine reality from our sight. That divine reality is not however lost to us. It is maintained by a loving Creator who waits for us to get so damned tired of this mess we made, that we seek Him out. And once we do, things start to change. Once we admit to ourselves that we cannot live a meaningful life without Him, the wall of illusion starts to crumble. Once we trust the divine over the sad and miserable things we put our trust in now, we start to see evidence of the truth. And that truth has nothing whatsoever to do with the things of this world. And despite our persistent belief that we can make the world better, we cannot but doubt the fallacy of the premise on which such a world is based. We have spent countless eonaeon trying to fix something that is based on an invalid assumption, namely that it is real! Once we challenge that assertion and open our minds to the possibility of another reality, we are shown a new world, a world long forgotten but of such beauty and peace that we are irresistibly drawn to it. The willingness of the soul to follow that attraction allows the recognition and acceptance of an increasingly persuasive reality.

I know of that reality. I lived in and accepted the world for many years until the aching of my soul and the pain of the material world drove me to find something better, and I did. The wondrous and unimaginable beauty that was exposed to me confirmed my direction and led me to a place where I no longer required speculation, proof, or even faith. It led me to a Mind and Spirit that welcomed, accepted, and rejoiced at my return. I have arrived at a juncture where I no longer need or accept any proof founded on the invalid premise of the material world. I know and I know that I know.

I am reminded of an incident with a former friend who nearly died in an automobile accident several years ago. She was in such serious condition that the doctors advised her children to come and see her because she would not make it through the night. She not only made it through the night but she survived and lived for many more years. She related to me how she had witnessed another world that was so real to her that, despite her family's and friends' scorn, she would never again believe in the reality of the world that took her husband's, and nearly her, life. And all this from a woman who was previously as entrenched in the material world as anyone I had known. That divine world exists, my friends. It has always existed and, once upon a time, we knew it and consciously lived in it.

A little over a year ago, my path finally led me to that same awareness. At that time, I started to receive poems that described my rediscovered truth. Since then, I have received over 700 of the most inspiring and hopeful poems I have ever read. And all that from a man who previously had never exhibited an ounce of creativity. But there's a good reason for that; it's not *my* creativity. The author of these poems lives in that place, the place we all came from, a place where I am now blessed to revisit from time to time. And on my increasingly frequent visits, I am honored to bring back these tiny bundles of joy, these celestial odes. I, like my reawakened friend, now believe in only one reality; the reality of a God-created world where we are invited back to be refreshed, to know truth again, and to make our Home. I have dedicated the remainder of my life to sharing these sneak peeks of that Home, in the hope that you will be as captivated by them as I am. Come with me now and let us seek our long lost Home together, that we may at long last, decline our living hell and relocate to our rightful place in the divine order. Let us fail to remember *The Great Forget* and accept instead the simple gold that is our heritage.

Peace's Wake

You present me, my Beloved
Such wonderful curiosities
To entertain and welcome my heart
It is all truly astounding
This procession I find myself part
The blessings just keep on coming
My life about to start
If this be foreboding of death
Then death I certainly partake
Yet I think it is but love offered
Offered in peace's wake

Children Must Sing

Children must sing
Of all their lovely things
Innocence remembered, not yet lost
Praising the unknown Source
Not knowing the impending cost
Their hearts must ring
The golden bell of love
They must laugh and sing
And hold, in hand, the ivory dove

My Only Pay

I face uncertainty now
The ego threatens with body as fool
I am confronted with mortality
To see what I will do

Fear besets me, I accept it not
For whatever befalls me
Must be my lot

I will not forsake my God
For He would never, to me, be far
He is my truth and reality
He is my comfort, my way
I admit no other to show me
Whether I go or stay

For if it is my time to go
I will leave behind what I may
My Home will welcome me shortly
The human form, my only pay

Mind Play

Let the body fade away
Into the nothingness it obeys
The Mind remains intact
Needing not a place to stay
Death consumes but the one
The other is God's to play

Wayne's Place

I recently visited Wayne's place
It is a room within my heart
Door closed from dusty things
Of which I have been apart

The story of Solomon took me there
Restored memories of golden days
When Wayne and I were befriended
By the oneness that came to stay

Even if but for awhile
Partners in crime, we were
Denying all the obvious
Laughing at the absurd
Elegant conversations
Plied at coffee's urn

Those wonderful, healing times
Were there to set me straight
And welcome back my brother
The one I could never hate

Though parted we were
By seamless time and space
In our hearts, we never left
Yet our lives would run a different race
Back in touch and touching
Our souls, within this place

A Willing Apprentice

A willing apprentice
I long to be
A neophyte in waiting
Yearning to be free

I could be led by no better
Nor taught quite as well
By my Brother, my Savior
My fortune He tells

Hand in hand with fate
He carries me far
He restoreth my soul
I am His willing apprentice
In the study of The Whole

Freed Mind

Stuck in a pigeon hole
For such a long time
All organized so neatly
Setup to fall in line
With the accepted way of thinking
Along the party lines

Accepting and assimilating
All of it put forth
By media, government, and demagogues
The law according to mediocrity
The brain without its source

Going along to get along
Afraid to rock the boat
Til it wrangled me to my roots
And grabbed me by my throat

Made me question everything
The common and the obscene
Turned my world upside down
To see what could be seen

The underbelly was displeasing
The fear and guilt unredeemed
But digging through the mud, I find
A tiny open seam
I unraveled and I parted it
To find a mind, now freed

Pile of Nothing

I am melted, simply melted
My head upon my knees
Slumped down into oblivion
To sample the aperitif
Melted, meaningless matter
To flow like baker's grease
Seeping between the floorboards
Flowing with the greatest of ease
Heading down and hell bound
Ending up in a pile of nothing
Back where once we were found

Hideous Deal

I know it's not real
I know it's not real
Much attention given
To approve your offered deal
I know you lie
You cheat and you steal
Pack up now and leave me
I decline the hideous deal

Clearly Insane

Oh my beloved
Green fields all
Diamonds never dimming
Prices that never fall
The cost of retention explained
But you've covered up the pain
By investing in unredeemables
The rationale found inane
Clearer vision is available
To see past the clearly insane

Trust and Such

Everything is in the eye of the beholder
The fullest range of thought
Yet applied to those outside of us
Paints the rose a dismal pot

Beauty, in the eye, it's true
Evil, sad to say, as well
Reviewing what we see in our brother
Can reflect as Heaven or hell

So be kind to the both of us
Treat us with gentle touch
For we judge or love each other
Based on the trust and such

To See Jesus

To see Jesus
See Him in your brother first
To see Jesus
Know His body was nothing
It was but to quench our thirst

For we need a form to acknowledge
That among us He stayed
When in truth, He has never left us
Only from our sight did He fade

Christ is who we look for
Jesus was just His form
He is as much in your brother
As inhabited the Hebrew form
We are a million more, or so
Of Christ in earthly norm

So look within, yourself and others
To see beyond the name
And know that Christ resides within
This simple earthly frame

Shows to Go You

I am reminded of a story, told on television of all places.
I have turned it to the poet's quill and here is how it goes.

A man waited on his rooftop
As the water rose round his home
He waited for God to rescue him

A small boat came by
And offered the man a ride
Yet he said, *No thank you*
I need no place to hide

A larger boat came roaring up
To offer the man some help
Yet he said, *No thank you*
I wait for my Savior to arrive

Soon, a helicopter flew over
And supplied the man a rope
Yet he said, *No thank you*
I haven't yet given up hope

The man drowned
And left for the Pearly Gates
And said, when he saw Jesus
What's the deal, you were much too late
Jesus said, *What the hell*
I sent several to delay your fate

It just shows to go you; fixed beliefs are not our friends.

The Real You

It's likely I will offend sensibilities
At least, I hope that's the case
I would hate to think I did all this work
And left out offense, in haste

I hope to rattle your cage
I desire to spin you around
My quest is to ignore you
Until the Real You comes to town

Hairy Toes

I am gifted continuously
The river that never slows
The love is streamed in sun rays
Upon my hairy toes
It tingles all the way to head top
My soul feels a tinkling too
The body dissolves, and I'm left with
The gift, of which I am imbued

Non Linear

Non acceptable linearity
It's what makes us tow the line
But it makes it a tad bit difficult
When you encompass all the lines
Existing everywhere and every time
No place we need not have abode
It's harder still to be linear
While trying to be The Whole

Kiva

Everyone is heard
When the circle is traversed in turn
Everyone gets their say
When all are held at bay

The Kiva, an ancient ritual
The object, its centerpiece
All for the divine allowing
Of communion to take place

So argue not, interrupt no more
Embrace the communication
Let it move us to more
More, in the way of oneness
Oneness, to make rich the poor

Weird Things Afloat

Weird things are afloat
They tilt and rock my boat
Waters shifting unpredictably
The tide holding my sway
We never know below us
Only the deeps can say
Yet whether shark or dolphin be
Only the deeps can say
But know we the sky above
And the gentle way it stays
Cooling and soothing our yesterday
It is the comforting way

Jesus et al

He wrote it
It's time to come out and say
That He wrote it
As if He were here today
Jesus Christ, as last well known
The one and only author
Of *The Course*, as it is known
Kind lady and brother intellectual
Converted atheists all
There but to hear and scribe the words
Left by Jesus et al

Time Trickery

Time trickery fooling with mind
It shows no absoluteness
It shows missing within the rhyme
A ticking and a tocking
Of eternity's endless clock
A tattoo of flimsy production
Overlaying the never-time stock
Past and future timed poorly
Unable to maintain or endure
There is but the single moment
The only tick-tock for sure

Virgin Spaces

Virgin pages
White and left alone
Possibilities still unlimited
Til grist for the holy tome
Sweet smell, unadulterated
Lines as silent as mime
Space still left for placement
Of words, ideas, and rhyme

500 Miracles

I have seen over 500 miracles
Immersed in love's sweet sway
Direct messages from Christ relayed

Yet I cling to fear's life vest
I cower to its power
Of which it doesn't own
The only power it uses
Bequeathed by my very loan
I have allowed the court jester
To displace his royal King
And assume the power throne

I think I've seen enough
Multi miracles to make my mind
I believe I will soon kick some butt
And leave sorry fear behind

Blank Pages Fade

It's wild and woolly out here
We never know what's coming next
It could be rice krispies
It could be our soul well vexed
We might need a hanky to cry
Our hearts may stir for a moment
We may end up laughing our butts off
Or pine for hero lost
We could end up shocked and dismayed
We might see a picture of Jesus
Or deny the couple getting laid
So if you deem to join me
And walk in this parade
Hold close and dear beside me
As we watch blank pages fade

Left in Rhyme

I require the courage of Christ
I invoke His presence somehow
A heavy burden must I lay down
All the fears that attend me now

I'm ready to make the leap
I'm ready to become disinvolved
With the ego and its minions
Upwards, my resolve

Time to claim my freedom delayed
Time to excavate the pain
Free myself of its properties
And lay waste to its chains

A lot is on the line here
A whole new world in time
In the world, not of it
I leave it in my rhyme

The Best of Games

I watched this team congeal
Saw them come together
Only to reveal
What lies beneath the sweat and tears
When one man bonds to another
And departs each other's fears

But now we see it
Play out on grander scale
The love between these men
Manifests the Holy Grail
This thing we call oneness
That forbade our boys to fail

I have seen them play
This most wonderful of games
The way it should be played
To take them to brotherly fame

Ask them how they feel
And surely they will say
The oneness that played between them
And brought them to this day

Go Rockies, stay strong and never fade
Love each other in playing
The very best of games

Love's Sweet Spot

Don't go future
Don't go past
Stand erect and be
In the moment that lasts
It is the point of concentration
It is the center spot
The only locale acceptable
To love's sweet lot

Simple to Mistake

Don't lean forward
Don't lean back
See what is before you
See what others lack
The truth is in the telling
The gift of it, to partake
The endless nature of it
Is simple to mistake

Separate Pawns

The preceding two poems
Belong as pair, they do
Appearing quite similar
In ways I never knew
They simply delivered that way
Not sure of the options foregone
They but weave into each other
To deny the separate pawn

Simple Appeals (To Be Free)

Simple appeals to God
Are enough requests for me
I long only to touch Him
And watch Him set me free

He is my Power and Source
I need nothing He does not give
His Life enables mine to live

His Will is mine
It is all I need
It consumes and triumphs me
To the point of being freed

We're Allowed

We're allowed to be imperfect here
Perfection grows not in stagnant ground
Our beneficence follows us closely
Til we hear the soliloquent sound
Yet never forget, my brother
We are conceived on holy ground
Enveloped in Perfection
In Christ reborn, we're found

Intelligence and Beauty

I am the imperceptible writer
I tell of wondrous, invisible things
Yet every now and then
Nature beholds me within
She shows me hawks a hovering
Mountains in ivory glaze
Sweet breezes gently touching
The mind within the maze
I am touched quite dearly
My heart seems unrestrained
My mind flows into the Other
Intelligence and beauty uncontained

Tell a Tall Tale

Tell a tall tale
Open the can
Let it swell
Growing to assume form
Loosing its mystic tell

A story emerges
It seems so real
Til we find the sacred ring
That makes it all disappear
Left with story-less truth
Assumed by that understanding
All known, beginning to end

Glory Found

Once we see Christ in each other
Is the day we see Him in ourselves
It is the day of total forgiveness
It brings the time to bear
When all is left, gone and senseless
Revealing the feast we share
Heaven found and rediscovered
The Home eternal bound
Beholding, as one, in each other
The vision complete and found

Heaven's Door

Behind the veil of condemnation
Lies pristine flowers arrayed
Arranged to be your point of promise
Where you see from prime perspective
All that lies ahead
The sweet truth, the simple I
Vision dancing in our heads
Revealing all that hatred hid
Closed heart and oneness shed
Lost years from loving God
Spent loving the self instead
Yet tarry not, it is real no more
Our Father waits expectedly
To join Him at Heaven's Door

Forgive

Forgive
Everyone
Everything

Love Proclaimed

On behalf of J&J Enterprises
I would like to present in whole
Our latest born to the family
Common Ground, the newest of tomes

Gestation was quite wonderful
Spiritual sex, before that, was sublime
Carrying the child full term
To deliver to the world on time

Some odes, some jokes, stories as well
All to bring us together
To weather the stormy swells

We'll keep on pumping out the pulp
Presenting words that wisely say
Jingles to jointly amuse us
Listening to what we pray

Hold tight to each other
Let but love live between
Let no one put asunder
What the poet and Lover proclaim

Collaborating With Christ

Collaborating with Christ
This is what I do
Requested, granted, and lived for
This is what comes through

Jesus is my buddy
He is my friend supreme
In Christ we are each other
There is no binding seam

We are one in the truest of senses
Indivisible, just like you
Come join the collaboration
No longer will One be two

How to Know

We all think we have
A corner on the truth
So how shall we decipher
That which arrives forsooth

Shall we judge by published doctrine
Shall we abide our parent's faith
Shall we accept that publicly offered
To take us to our fate

I know of few rules to know
Yet these I hold to my heart
I know if my Master tells me
And it doesn't make me fart

Christ at the Halfway

We have laughed together
And cried together
Coming apart at the seams
Yet as one we stayed
No matter what it seemed

We love each other, my brother
He is the greatest of friends
He is the Christ unfabricated
To attend our souls within

No need to seek without
No reason to hide within
Meeting Christ at the halfway
He will lead us to Heaven then

Tiny Bundles

I am the stork
Delivering babies
Making them
Having them
Giving them away
Citizens of the world, they be
Tiny bundles for all to see

Two Inch Repent

A two inch repent
Is all I see sent
Not much of anything to repeal
Only my mind that is bent
I have done nothing, in truth
To require my consent
I originate as holy
Part of God I am
Nothing to be ashamed of
Nothing to deny
A mistake once made
Is so easily forgiven
Yet to perpetuate it is pain
Forgetting truth in the process
Keeping us locked insane
But what we are is what we are
No matter the guise or frame
Accept what is, deny the false
With God and Christ
We are the same

It's Just a Horse

It's just a horse, of course
Four legs to propel our fate
It's just a horse, of course
To get us somewhere too late
The journey but measures zero
No here to there to please
Little transportation needed
To take us to holy peace
The body, the form, the frame
Embraced to lead us again
From here to there, for nothing
Stand but straight and tall, and still

All to Whom We Relate

The most wonderful moments of my life
Have been spent with You in unison
The moments two became One

All is gone to delay our plan
We become the essence of each other
Few will likely understand

But come their day, they will
I will be there to open the gate
Like those who came before me
All to whom we relate

Alone in the Park

Alone in the park
All appearing quite stark
Tis snowing and raining
And whatever else
Colors this dismal day
Yet nothing about it saddens me
I am in the expectant way
Never alone in the park again
Present in a holy way

The Call

I come to you, my brother
Baring heart, open and wide
Offering to share the Christ with you
Let us meet up close inside
It is free, forever, and love
This bond that answers us all
Never have I wanted such oneness
Til I knew it from The Call

Holy Say

There's just too much pressure
To be this or that
Too much acquiescence
Too much primal fat

The search continues
The looking here and there
The ever present Presence
Eluded, somehow, my stare

Ask the question
Hold thought at bay
Await directions to follow
Listen for the Holy Say

Goodbye to Tyrants

I sense I am falling into disfavor
With tiny ruler of kingdom of air
Sensing a bit of rejection
Knowing the real Kingdom is there
I go where it cannot
To become again, part of The Whole
I give him leave quite shortly
To let go his hold on my soul
I need no lingering duality
My part is now The Whole
Completely indifferent to separation
It cannot reside in the fold
We stand together
Not separate, but One
Saying goodbye to tyrants
Standing together, in the Son

That Loving Thing

I like the no-thing
It's akin to what I bring
A notion of nothing
Can make my heart sing
All One, no place or thing
All for the love of oneness
All for that loving thing

Shuckin and Jivin

We've been shuckin and jivin so long
We've lost the authentic way
Got carried away by our bad selves
Sucked in through the fray
It's time we dressed down to nothing
Get bare and leave it behind
Come gently into each other
Give praise to nothing sharp
No more shuckin and jivin
We dance the Paradise Harp

Disconnected Pieces

We dare not connect images
By nature, alone and discrete
Born apart, not of oneness
Destined for eventual defeat

A lie gives away false light
Paints a picture dimly lit
Trying to connect false images
All so improperly fit

Let go the effort
To continue is clearly insane
Never mind disparate pieces
They are lies, and illusion, and pain

Telling of Holy Heart

The poems make me breathe
Life back into the ode
Both existing together
No boundaries to forebode
I am them, they are me
Some still likely potential
The rest are meant to be
A single solidarity emerges
The words no longer apart
Poems and poet are one
Telling of the Holy Heart

Extraneous Bull

Pray you enter here, let's talk
Numerous extraneous disturbances
May interfere, if we allow it so
Or cut right to the core of it
And say what we truly know
Zip right through the bullshit
Let us relate as we might
We are brothers and sisters together
And live we in the light

Mind Fences

Argue enough for your limitations
And surely they will be yours[1]
Fight enough to make them real
Reality then, becomes the fight
Regardless the tender appeal
All limits, be they none
Are self-imposed, at least
Lay them down, let them go
Watch mind fences so decrease

1. Lines 1 & 2 from "Illusions, The Adventures of a Reluctant Messiah" by Richard Bach

The Greater

Crudeness, is in the eye, baby
That beholds the lesser fruit
All seen is mind-born first
The cause of lesser loot

To know within, the cause of pain
Courageous enough to deal it
The dead man loser's hand

When light appears unsheathed
And evicts the lesser way
The mind will come alive at last
In its greater Home, to stay

Warm Snow

Crystalline warm snow
Never melting, ever-flow
Beauty and purity unmatched
It shows us the ever-know
A place so clean and white
Yet warming our very soul
No room left for eternity
Consumed by the ever-so

Contact

Contact has been made
Residing in the public domain
Fingertips lightly touching
Extensions of the Holy Main
Brothers recognizing brothers
Resembled by the sweet refrain
Of voices singing love songs
To alleviate the pain
Bringing healing to each other
Soothing the brother-mind
Finally coming together
To play among the rhyme

Rhythm Into Rhyme

I have a sort of rhythm
That comes from writing these lines
Streaming somewhere in the ether
I pick up on it, from time to time
It modulates these arrangements
It makes them hum in time
Permeating their very essence
Turning rhythm into rhyme

Simple Man

I'm a simple man at heart
I belch and burp
And sometimes fart
Yet I know a good deal when I see one
A simple, loving complexity
Obviates the obvious norm
No matter what we do here
No matter the fate or form
All of the form's feeble fumblings
Cannot deny who we are
Christ, one and all
Born of the Holy Star

Invisible Beauty

He's got me farting
In the same book, *twice*!
I'm not sure I like the image
Doesn't make me seem very nice

I will say as some defense
The feat rarely done in public
My daddy gave me more sense

Regardless, let's dissolve that image
Of man and gas adjoined
Realize the form reviewed
Is but a two-tailed coin

Images are all deceiving
Misdirecting to flatter planes
Reflection, oh so blinding
Trying to see, in vain

Let nothing the body offers
Deter you in the least
Nor images false of brotherhood
That shows the hairy beast

Instead, look upon your brother
As light, and love, and one
See only invisible beauty
In divine form of Son

Paradise Stay

Purification in non-standard form
Snow white for the eyes to see
Yet cleansing beyond the borders
Of where our minds can be

Out here, the reflection sings
Its minute version of the song
Seeing only what gets away
And what had set me wrong
Back now, from its premise
I won't stay around very long

I wait for the inflection
To carry me far away
From this too-confined time-space
Home, to Paradise stay

Chiming Rhyme

My job is to say a lot with a little
To manage an economy of words
Stringing them together so cleverly
Til they sound like something I've heard
When it resonates with my spirit
When it fits within my mind
The message now primed to deliver
To result in chiming rhyme

Bet Your Life

The body has no dignity
A cover-up is the best we can do
We hide its dirty little secrets
To appear as though we knew
Of a higher decorum of mind
Of a grace that obviates the form
Of a state that does not preclude
All that eludes the norm

We do such things as all know
Yet admit them not as known
The cover-up is planned
As we sit upon the throne

So look your best, my friend
Ignore the body's faults
But don't bet your life upon it
For your life will surely halt
And when the body betrays you
Turn to the Mind that will not

Brothers in Cause

The moment you give up on separation
Is the time to rejoin The Whole
Occasion to lay down the baser things
And take ownership of your soul

Let us be together again
Let our lines dissolve in space
It's time to be whole again
Time to conclude the race

You've arrived, if you believe it
You're there, if memory be yours
Only to let go of fantasy
To see beyond the form

Gather your lovers before you
Assemble them, brothers and sisters all
The fare is but so little
It's hard to understand the pause
But one of these days, we'll know them
As love and brothers in cause

Ego Perch

I neither need it nor heed it
The fear that makes this call
I know well of its parentage
And from whence it got its balls

But as darkness leaves the room
As light's arrival is made
So shall fear seek refuge
When truth no longer fades

It is but part of the illusion
It partners with rage and shame
They cohabit to think of ways
To put someone else to blame

They are deceitful and alone
Disconnected from their home
Destined to fade into nothing
As love brings justice along

The goal, to be left with nothing
Which obscures or delays our search
Nothing, which is all it is
Time to deny its perch

My Friend the Atheist

Dear brother, who does not believe
Settles for the table laid
If you don't believe in Heaven
The alternative becomes your fate
That option, my friend
Bargains for the little you have
Argues for its impotent sincerity
All that the senses made
A paltry table indeed
A meal of dubious test
If you must believe in something
Let it not be this lonely mess
Open your mind instead
To the daily given bread
Dare to see beyond appearances
To Paradise that waits instead

Father's Words

My goal is to never deny it
The impulse to words supplied
The thing that brings me such joy
And convinces me He never lied
For the Brother who is my need
Is my benefactor as well
He loves me in the gentlest of ways
And gives terms to Creator's Will

No Need of Glasses

I take off my glasses
So I may truly see
All that mitered glass
Refused to put before me
All that eyes would tell
Of obvious featured hell
Blind me to the vision
The path before me laid
I have no need of glasses
I proceed blind and unafraid

Divine Attention

To whatever you give your attention
Will become alive to you
Be it false god or Heaven
It will bring a bill past due
Pay the one in dollars
Or painful body gain
Or settle up with our Father
And behold the Heavenly refrain

Just Lucky I Guess

I'm just lucky, I guess
A lot continues to happen
Of which I must profess
I gave my life to my Beloved
Mind and soul, of intent
I have since to lose a bit
Of His blessings daily sent
My life is so different
Than, for eons, I insisted it be
Having now sweetly released it
A new one, eternal, I see
God's love is not a false promise
I now feel it every day
More real than any expected
When we left His side that day
He simply waits and loves us
Until we find our way

Sweet Days

Sweet days, such sweet days
When my Brother comes to visit
In His gentle loving way
He abides with and in me
He knows just what to say
Becoming my breath and spirit
To show me in every way
That what He says is real
In those lovely lines we pray
And in those sweet days before us
In which we joyfully play

A Very Good Cause

When I turned my life over to Jesus
When I allowed the Christ to be
He warned me I might get silly
For all the world to see
Normally, that would rock my boat
Normally, I'd get choked up and pause
But this time around, I'm okay with it
It's all for a very good cause

He Had to Die

It was required that He die
To come back through resurrection
And show that death was a lie
That no matter the pain or strife
That flails upon our soul
There is always life to live
Despite the seeming hole
We disappear as in an eye wink
Here today, gone an instant more
The illusion cuts out from view
Life forevermore

Hungry Still

Take as much fruit as you can eat
Yielded by the Tree of Life
Take in as much as mind allows
Towards vision of the Heavenly life
And when that revelation appears
Absorb, let it all sink in
For to eat of the Tree of Life
Is to feast, as one, within
And in that divine place of dining
Your brothers surround your place
All meeting up together
To see His Holy Face
To take in one last view
Dining done, we leave our place
But hunger you will again
For the feast that forever fills
You will return to His table
And disappear, hunger stilled

The Chef and the Sailor

Stories, gross and glory
These are my words, so far
I experience no limits imposed
Other than the ones I bar

Jumping between truth and illusion
Is likely freaking some out
I'm sorry, I don't make the menu
I simply serve what is lying about

The Chef, far wiser than me
My Captain, a far better sailor
Than ever I could be
I'm only along for a ride and a meal
And to see what all I can see

On All Fours

He walks to her on all fours
This tiny little boy at park
He's trying to the give the dog a break
And let him know *his* bark
Exploring fresh snow off beaten path
Ignoring mommy's pleas
Life is too short, and he knows it
To do as others please
Living in the moment
The joy from that single act
Mommy has lost sight of something
To the boy, a simple fact
To be happy, be in the moment
Never give way to fear
Laugh in the face of disaster
Knowing that love is near
Perhaps mommy will learn some day
Perhaps a child she will become
Saying to hell with the beaten path
And depart to rejoin the One

God Being God

We may call It by disparate names
Creativity or even Love
It all but remains the same
It fits us like a glove
The extending of the universe
Love unbounded at last
Tis holy it is, my brother
No matter the color it's cast
It is God being God
Holiness, forever to last

Simply in the Present

Forgive the past
Let go the future
Stand with Christ in this spot
The past is surely gone
The future belongs to God
Live simply in the present
It's the only time we've got

The Words I Say

I don't decide what is written
It is too fine to restrain
Holy profound explanations
Run amok with crudeness untamed

All have a point to make
All are part of the plan
Above my mind to know
Or hope to understand

I accept it as is, it is holy
I dare not delay the plan
My fingers shall never betray me
No matter on the words I stand

If it riles you, pay attention
A lesson is there to be learned
A trifling bit of unforgiveness
That somehow we thought we earned

So pay close attention, my brother
They all will point the way
I dare not do the pointing
I'll merely get in the way

So write I will, unabashed
And Christ, my muse, will stay
Whatever moves my pen along
And bids me point His way

This Day

Dear J, we have had ourselves a day
This shower of love between us
Has come, once more, to stay
Writing as one together
We bring the song to play
Upon our mystical instruments
To sing in a holy way
We've delivered a few this morning
I don't know what else to say
I thank You and I love You
For giving us this day
(Fifteen have come to stay)

Guilt's On You

To be perfect
It needed to contain
The idea of imperfection
To be whole
It needed to encompass
The separated soul

The apple, the icon
Of the thought entertained
It came before the arrival
Of Adam/Eve's looming bane
They are the halves
Of the separated whole
After the idea was imbibed
They split into separate souls
Blaming each other ever since
To defend the fragmented whole

The guilt of blowing it
We pass from self to self
Unable to bear the lonely pain
We give it to someone else
Over and over, we go
The guilt's on you, don't you know

One More Fence

The pain of accepting separation
The notion of what I had done
Is too much, I cannot retain it
I'll give to you, dear one

Yet now you look quite guilty
I don't know if you can be trusted
Perhaps I must restrain
Any viable offer of friendship
And challenge if you be sane
For if I cannot trust you
And guilty you appear to be
I better take arms against you
So you don't put your guilt on me

Keep you at bay, I will
Forget that *brother* nonsense
Clearly split and loving it
The world gets another fence

Loss of Love

The release from guilt masks as pleasure
It's a secret we are sworn to keep
For to give up that we treasure
Is a price deemed far too steep
Yet the other side of that coin
Is the pain which breeds in its keep
Giving the guilt to our brother
Or sister to take inside
Is a pleasure only in dreaming
The double-edged sword does slide
Right between our divided heart
To pierce our swollen pride
For if we cannot love each other
Pleasure and pain aside
Then we do not love ourselves
Loss of love is too great to abide

Until I Go

I wanted to be an architect
I became a geek instead
Tried my hand at leadership
Kept me going for awhile
One night I became poet
An assent from that day on
Gifts bestowed as blessings
To share and then let go
My life now spent in peace
Until the time I go
I know I know

All We Can Be

We're so much more beautiful together
Than all the parts on display
Overwhelm our hearts, it would
If only we could see what I say
It is just now dawning to me
It is love, I wish to share it
To make us all we can be

Holy Grace

I don't know what I know
I haven't even a clue
All this crap around me
Is making it hard to eschew

I would like to depend on something
That doesn't let me down
Nothing here fits that bill
I'm off to track it down

Knowledge, I know, lives somewhere
I just need to find that place
I'm hoping to get educated
By the light of Holy Grace

Wayne and Solomon

Wayne and Solomon, both came through
The brothers drew nearer to me
As the tale became truth
Just as told to be

My dear old friend named Wayne
And my eternal Brother in Christ
Wayne and Solomon in welcome
Bring treasures of mind to apprise
Many more than story told
Far exceeding its tiny size
Treasure disbelieved but wanted
These two kind souls, my prize

As others fall away for a moment
I treasure the ones that stay
The journey becomes far lighter
Than any alone we make

Names will change
People will come and go
But Christ will meet me in unison
No matter where I go

I invite these two friends to join me
As we travel the length of this day
Soon to become one together
Walking the love lit way

Center Spot

Everyone has lost their bottoms
Their tops, too far away to see
Still searching for the middle
Finding the sweet spot, indeed
Looking for a center
A spot to settle down
No more bobbing and weaving
One place to spread around
A spot of stillness bound
There to see my Savior
In eye of brother found

Separate Thoughts

We have the same goals
We come from the same Whole

Love is the oneness we crave

Separation is cracks in our back
Gaps between us
That love cannot intrude upon

Work it with the right demographic

I live here only in this moment

Snapshots through the rear window
That's what the world is

It's a no-brainer, baby
To give your life to God

Get thee behind me, satan
Let your fear never darken my door
I leave you behind forever now
I subscribe to welcoming moors

This is my way, I am certain now

You see far more, Beloved
Your eyes, the distance please

It's no contest, baby
All this for That

We are part of a Whole that includes us all
It takes us to a place of truth
A place not remembered here

I never thought of such love, such joy

This work matters
My brothers matter

Never have I known such peace as this moment

My Father's Will is my will

Zap, zap, here today, gone tomorrow

My Father's Will is my will

Alone has nothing to do with the body

Who would have thunk it
The kid from Flint

Look at yourself as you're angry
Look at yourself as you fade

I've got to let go of that
It's nothing, as well

Dream director, it's my role
Keeps me apart from The Whole

Prose flows, poems bloom
Let's call it work, if we have to

Christ available through these gifts

The hole is filled by The Whole

It takes me to that poetic place

Is judgment inherent to the conversation

I've been there, done that
How can I judge my brother

I think, my Friend, You've done it again

All That Lasts/Critical Mass

If we fail to share
And decline each other so
Then where is *The Course* in this
Where does its spirit go

The only viable approach there be
Is to live and love together
In Christ, our Home to see

Oneness is all there is
The rest, just ice on the glass
All else leaves us with nothing
So what, we're at critical mass
So what, we have all that lasts

Undying Life

The truth of the reality is
This reality has no truth
A jigsaw lens before us
Seen through sightless eyes

Yet if blindness is all you see
The only color is black
And see we not, in darkness
The light must bring us back

I know it seems quite real
The touch, the sound, the smell
But question its divine feasibility
And ask what it truly tells

If this be real, then God help us
For surely we will die
Do peel the smoggy layers
To see what doesn't lie

To find a truth worth finding
A treasure worthy of us all
Look not with eyes or ears
Peer through the darkened pall

Ask God what is real and needed
To live a happy life
Look for invisible beauty
Look for undying life

A Fifty Year Affair

A fifty year affair with baseball
Why so much love for the game
Why does it resemble my soundings
When I followed it not to fame

I guess it's the accord of the matter
The powerful ebb and flow
As ball and man together
Make it happen swiftly so

A game of speed and power
Of finesse and hectic calls
The only game brighter than baseball
Has yet to hear my call

Finer Direction

We get finer direction as we go
At first, a broad map is fine
Ask and receive what is necessary
To travel our destined line

Sooner or later, we'll get there
A Place where all will be fine
A Place of endless possibility
A position to obviate time

Eventually, to release it
A time to truly let go
The momentum and attraction will take us
To path at end, and Home

Fit In

My soul has become much larger
Larger enough to take in my kin
Large enough to fit in
Into a context much grander
Than ever I've been in

The rate, I believe, is accelerating
I should likely strap myself in
It should be a blast of revelation
Turning my attention within

Restored to my original size
Has reminded me of my Home
Back to the birth of innocence
The one I left when unatoned

I'm knocking at that door again
Asking to be remembered in
As in, "Sure, I remember you"
"Come on in"

Only in the Moment

Don't let sleeping dogs lie
Kick em in the ass
We've slept for countless eons
A long and lengthy past

Just thank God you've heard the word
That puts you past its reach
The sullied part, resolve yourself
By listening to those who teach

Know by watching lies pale and fade
They are but shadow with no future play
Now we put the past behind us
Solely in Holy Instants, do we stay

The Forgiving Song

I know you are in pain
Death beckons and makes you afraid
But know that God is ever present
He is your ultimate fate

The disease is but an indication
Of the decay of unresolved hate
Let go the life that plagues you
Learn to forgive before it's too late

Ask Christ, He will direct you
Bid you arise and come along
As He guides you in loving ways
And teaches the forgiving song

Love Lying at My Feet

I have long been the loner
The one who stands apart
Hoping to find safety in numbers
Numbers that stole my heart

Alone and lonely
Thought my brother was too
Redirected to thoughts of separation
Believing that one was two

Defending and striking beforehand
Just in case I might be attacked
Causing oneness to retract
Leaving me in retreat
Leaving love lying at my feet

Lost and Found

Remove the chastity board
Let the gap be swept away
It is but a thing of dreams
It has no reason to stay

The gap that lies between us
Is only in our minds
It hides the fear of joining
That sneaks up from behind

In truth, there is no division
It is just our way to hide
From the truth of ever oneness
And the fear of God inside

Fear not, my brother
That without it, you will be lost
I have been in love's embrace
To be there involves no cost

In fact, it is just the opposite
We are immersed in love's sweet sound
No one is ever lost there
Only our Home is found

Nowhere Else to Be

Christ has come
He has always been here
Oneness arrives
Where it lives eternal
God has appeared
Where He cannot but be
Love knocks and advises
Of the arrival of all three
Yet it is not They who come
They stay where They have been
There is no place without Them
There is no room for sin
It is we who have not been here
When in truth, we could never leave
It is the truth of oneness
There is nowhere else to be

Sweet Terms

I am a layered man
I see now the destined plan
Some damn nice work went on here
To make me become this man
Sixty years in the making
Lots of twists and turns
A bumpy ride at times
The rest had all sweet terms

I see now things that remind me
Of how and why I am here
Things planned for eons
To prepare me for being clear
Clear enough to do what I do
To prepare these given pages
Everything needed to arrive here
To revel among the sages

The bumpy ride is over
I come now to take my turn
To make right the trusted agenda
Doing it on Heavenly terms

The Offer

Be healed and heal
The call I am hearing now
An offer generous and appealing
But I don't yet see how
A bona fide offer, though unsure
I'm a little new at this game
I know it is wholly genuine
I know it offers me fame
Not quite sure if I reckon it
How or why I'll be there
All I know is of the offer
And within it, we all may share

The Poem Before Me

This, you might find quite startling
I'll have to say, I do too
But I have my share of maladies
More than one or two
Let's take a minute and consider them
It's a long list, you'll agree
Headaches, arthritis, and soreness
Compete with blood pressure too steep
A little trouble breathing at times
My legs have numbness, they do
All these and more, they plague me
Yet I never get sick with the flu
So you see, I'm really quite healthy
How fit can a person be
On second thought, I might take the offer
Presented by the poem before me

Betrayal

The body still seeks to betray me
But guiltless, in truth, it is
It is but the goal of projection
To cover it with lots of sin

So look to my mind, I will
Cry out for revelation to be
Determine the source of the ailments
That persist in plaguing me

I pray the healing offer to arrive
I long for its tender embrace
My Lord will bestow upon me
All to be restored by faith

Katrina

Death and devastation
Bred in pitiless form
The worst that life has to offer
In the face of perilous storm

The tragedy fueled by indifference
Compassion had fled the scene
We forgot to take care for each other
We forgot what love means

The pain and suffering and despair
All because we were not there
To hold and comfort each other
To survive the violent snare

This disaster, among others
Shows us what ego declares
When we lose sight of each other
And forget, for our brother, to care

If you think this will change, you're wrong
It will continue to tear us apart
Until we reject separation
Let oneness rule our hearts

I'll Miss You Bobby

I'll miss you when you go, Bobby
Your strange looks and awkward wit
But mainly because you see the world
Yet remained not full of it

The sweet twang of your guitar
The penetrating tone of the harp
And oh, those words
And the way you sing

"I'll be in your dream"
"If you let me be in yours"

My God, they land in my soul
Be they the poet's or the fool's
Either way, they often rang true

We rode the same train of thought
For years, the trail led on
We grew old together, my friend
I'll miss you when you're gone

Declining World

In a world where homes decline
And vehicles decline
And bodies decline
I have a tough time, sometimes
With a world in such decline

How do we settle for this
Why do we deem ourselves little
Why not insist on better
Than this pathetic, declining riddle

I suppose it's here for the taking
Or better, for letting go
If something offends thee, my brother
Refuse to let it be so

Decline no more, fellow earthling
To give away all that bears
The mark of unmistakable misery
For the route to Heaven-bound stairs

Holy Pull

I'm always looking for a better way
To make myself a better day
One in which little gets in my way

A notch above, one rung more
If I keep climbing this ladder
I'll likely stop getting sore
About all those little things
That rubbed me wrong before

It's our mind, we can change it
It's our life, we can save it
But we'll need to do it together
All of us, to do our part in it

For it is one mind and life we save
When we dare to stand tall
The separated isn't worth the saving
It amounts to nothing at all

So look for the better way
Insist on the higher ground
A way and place that enjoys us
As we appear in the soul well found

Be simple, be honest
More than your self, it's true
Declare independence from form
Wait for the Holy Pull to ensue

Plato's Cave #2

We are prisoners in so many ways
Locked up without recognition
On multiple recurrent days
When Plato's cave is all we see
We go blind in so many ways
Let's face it, but please don't admit it
We see so little these days

Time to get honest with numero uno
Take pause to open that gate
Be willing to face yourself, my friend
And exit that lonely cave

It's much better out here
I never liked it much in there
Way too much guilt and fear
I'm likely more headed where
I can free myself from this blindness
And see myself in the clear

Prodigal Thought

Lost in our own minds
Where else would we be
Certainly not gone from Heaven
Home of the original We

Born in Eden, never to leave
But flight of fancy took us away
While we remained where we lived
A disconnected idea that strayed
Took flight away from Home
Leaving its Master lonely
For the one that got away

Errant thought became our domain
A home away from Home
We left, yet we stayed
The thought left for earth
While our truth remained

Better Half

Who is she or he
The love of your life
The one you seek to complete you
The one who will be your wife

Will he be what you need
Will she bring you back to life
Will she be your better half
Will he enrich your life

This other half, this missing piece
That holds and attracts your mind
Will they truly love you
Will they be true and kind

I'm not sure how to break the news
But two halves do not make a whole
Each half is but an illusion
That, for a time, steals our soul

Wholeness can never be divided
To appear as separate parts
No matter how much he appeals you
A half can't restore your heart

Take another view of your brother
Or sister, as the case may be
Know you are each The Whole
You need only this to see

The Day You Stay

Thank you, J
I cherish it when you come this way
Even if but for a moment
I love what you have to say

You daily surprise me
You divine jokester, you
Always ready to astonish
Forever your words ring true

They may be ode or fable
They may go deep within
They may be dark or golden
They bring love denying sin

Either way, you always refresh me
Bringing proof of the Heavenly way
You are my friend and lover
I pray for the day you stay

www.ingramcontent.com/pod-product-compliance
Lightning Source LLC
Chambersburg PA
CBHW060404090426
42734CB00011B/2254